Preface

The following pages are designed to celebrate equally the Tradescant family, especially John Tradescant the Elder and his son John the Younger, master gardeners to the Crown of England and avid collectors of all sorts of 'rarities', and Elias Ashmole, royalist, herald, astrologer, antiquary and collector, through whom the Tradescant collections came to the University of Oxford. There they constituted the foundation which became, after the formal visit of the Duke of York (later James II) on 21 May 1683, the first institutional museum in Britain open to the public. That museum in Oxford still opens to the public; it still bears Ashmole's name.

The Tradescant rarities, or at least a nucleus of the less perishable items, survive, and have recently been installed in a specially designed setting in the Ashmolean, and fully published in an extensive and learned catalogue, *Tradescant's Rarities*, edited by the author of this booklet. So equipped, the former contents of 'Tradescant's Ark' should survive the flood of time for another three hundred years. The Tradescant family's holding of plants, that flourished in their garden at Lambeth, has however long since vanished, though their name still clings to that popular house-plant *Tradescantia*. The revival of the Tradescant memory at St. Mary's at Lambeth is therefore all the happier in the tercentenary year of Ashmole's translation of their collections to his museum.

The elaborate T[...] churchyard is famous, a[...] setting that would hav[...] seventeenth century, l[...] volunteers. The garden [...] H M The Queen Mothe[...] [...]nce the Vice-Chancellor of the University of Oxford, attended by his Bedel with his mace, the two Proctors, the Director of the Ashmolean Museum and Mr Arthur MacGregor, all suitably robed, laid a wreath on the tomb of the Tradescants, and then, within the church, a second wreath on the grave slab of Elias Ashmole, buried there on that same date 291 years before.

Sir David Piper
Director of the Ashmolean Museum,
Trustee of the Tradescant Trust.

I

Tradescant the Elder: a career in the making

The final decades of Elizabeth I's reign witnessed the birth of John Tradescant the elder, although the place and date of his birth are as uncertain as his parentage is obscure. Anthony Wood's claim that Tradescant was a Dutchman has never been disproven, but it has lost support since the discovery of namesakes among 16th-century parish registers in Suffolk and it is to there that his origins are currently ascribed.

On 18 June 1607 Tradescant firmly enters the historical record as a young man on his wedding day. The ceremony was held at Meopham in Kent: the bride was Elizabeth Day, daughter of a former vicar of the parish, and the groom a gardener aged about thirty. Two years elapse before a name can also be given to his employer, but by that time he had secured an enviable position in the service of Robert Cecil, 1st Earl of Salisbury. Having recently exchanged his mansion at Theobalds for Hatfield House in Hertfordshire, Salisbury had assembled a talented team of craftsmen to transform it to his liking: while squads of builders, plasterers and painters laboured to beautify the house, the parklands in which it lay were remodelled by Mountain Jennings and the gardens revolutionized by John Tradescant.

Plants to match this ambitious undertaking were not to be found in England and to meet the Earl's exacting tastes Tradescant was dispatched on a botanical shopping spree which must have made him the envy of his contemporaries. From the bills he ran up — still preserved at Hatfield — Tradescant's progess can be traced through Flushing, Middelburg, Rotterdam and Delft, to Leiden and Haarlem. The lists of purchases tell of tulips and anemones, currants and vines, and above all fruit trees — apricots, quinces, cherries, pears, medlars, and many others. A bill for 2 guineas shows that these Dutch prizes were shipped from Brussels to Hatfield,

Gardener carved on the staircase at Hatfield House, traditionally identified as John Tradescant the Elder.

while Tradescant himself journeyed on to Paris. There, in the company of the ambassador's gardener, he scoured the city for still more plants worthy of his grand scheme at Hatfield. Amongst other purchases, he bought from Jean Robin, *herboriste* to the French court, pomegranates, figs and other trees, and was given 'manye other Rare Shrubs' out of friendship and admiration. That winter over one thousand specimens found their way back to Hatfield, many of them previously unrecorded in England.

Although the fruits of this and other collecting expeditions have become part of our common inheritance, not a single tree survives which was planted by Tradescant's hand. Something of them may yet be seen, however, in a manuscript in the Bodleian Library, Oxford, entitled 'Tradescant's Orchard'. The belief that this was intended to serve as a guide to the gardens at Hatfield is now questioned, but there is at least one undoubted connection: amongst some 65 varieties of fruit illustrated in the manuscript along with their dates of ripening, is one designated 'the Amber Plum which J. T. as I take it brought out of France and groweth at Hatfield'.

Tradescant's career with the Salisburys continued with the 2nd Earl, who succeeded his father in 1611. Under him the gardens at Salisbury House in the Strand were much improved and work was undertaken on other family properties. In this context a bill has been noted among the Salisbury manuscripts relating to a visit to Cranborne by Tradescant in November 1610, in order to plant trees.

The amber plum from 'Tradescant's Orchard'

3

From Canterbury to Barbary

Midsummer of 1615 saw Tradescant in a new post as gardener at St. Augustine's Palace at Canterbury. Formerly a property of the Salisburys, St. Augustine's had been bought in 1612 by Lord (formerly Sir Edward) Wotton, a politician, diplomat, and considerable scholar.

Once again Tradescant proved a credit to his master. Sir Henry Mainwaring journied to Canterbury 'to see my Lord Wottons garden and to confer with his Gardener' over the cultivation of melons; John Parkinson, in his day the principal authority in England on botanical matters, made careful note of the exotics which flourished there, including varieties of mandrakes, garlic and wild pomegranates, the latter 'never seene in England, before John Tradescante my very loving good friend brought it from the parts beyond the Seas'.

Tradescant's travels from Canterbury took him to regions where strange peoples and unfamiliar plants vied for his attention. From the first of these journeys, during which he accompanied Sir Dudley Digges in 1618 on an embassy to Muscovy via the North Cape, there survives a veritable treasure in the form of Tradescant's diary. The contents of the diary, preserved in the Bodleian Library, accurately mirror its author's insatiable curiosity. On the voyage from Gravesend to Archangel, he made notes of the wind and tide, the appearance of landmarks, sea birds and whales — even the daily menu. Once landed, every custom of the local inhabitants was subjected to his scrutiny, as were, of course, the details of the local vegetation. Many of the berries gathered from the Russian countryside were painstakingly nurtured on the voyage home, while others were dried on the spot and the seed sent as gifts to like-minded gardeners. There were also roses in abundance, said by those who had (unlike Tradescant himself) 'the sence of smelling', to be 'marvelus sweete'.

Tradescant's field observations represent the first botanical records ever made on Russian soil and several introductions resulted from the expedition. On Parkinson's authority we have the names of two species observed or introduced by 'that worthy, curious and diligent searcher and preserver of all natures rarities and varieties' namely white hellebore and purple crane's bill.

'Male and female mandrakes', a favourite botanical curiosity, by Jacob Meydenbach.

4

Russian counting-frame or abacus from the Tradescant Collection in the Ashmolean Museum.

Amongst the varieties later grown at Lambeth was a rose designated the *Rosa Moscovita*, perhaps another trophy, while the museum which later bore Tradescant's name boasted the 'Duke of Muscovy's vest wrought with gold upon the breast and armes'. A small Russian counting-frame — the earliest surviving example of such a thing — is still displayed in the Tradescant Gallery at the Ashmolean Museum.

The blockade of Algiers in the years 1620-21 provided the second opportunity for Tradescant to exchange the quiet of the Canterbury flower beds for a whiff of adventure and a taste of botanical novelty.

Joining the pinnace *Mercury* as a gentleman-volunteer, Tradescant spent some seven months at sea with the fleet. Sadly, there are no detailed accounts of his personal adventures on this occasion, although secondary sources hint at opportunities grasped for botanising: the 'Algiers apricot' is said to owe its introduction to this bellicose expedition, as is *Trifolium stellatum*, the starry-headed clover, brought from Formentera in the Balearic Islands. Other souvenirs may be represented among the 'Moores dagger', 'Barbary Spurres pointed sharp like a Bodkin', and similar rarities which were later displayed in the 'Ark'.

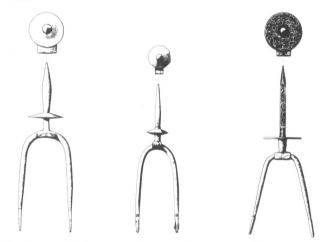

Tradescant's 'Barbary Spurres pointed sharp like a Bodkin'.

5

Keeper of His Majesty's Gardens, Vines and Silkworms

If success had smiled on Tradescant's career to date, from 1623 it was to be crowned with a whole series of achievements. In this year he entered the service of George Villiers, Duke of Buckingham, the most powerful voice in the land. Further visits had to be made to the Low Countries for trees to clothe Buckingham's parks and gardens, notably at Newhall in Essex, but the Duke evidently recognized more valuable talents and, perhaps, congenial company in the person of his gardener. When Buckingham himself was sent to Paris in 1625 to carry home Henrietta Maria as the bride of Charles I, Tradescant was entrusted with 'My Lords stuff Trunks &c' — no doubt the wardrobe of stunningly lavish clothes in which Buckingham won the hearts of all Paris. Amid the celebrations, which went on for several weeks, Tradescant found time to gather a further £120 worth of trees and flowers, most probably from the Paris nurserymen who were already numbered among his friends.

In less favoured times, too, Tradescant was to be found at Buckingham's side, as on the disastrous expedition of 1627 which laid siege to the Isle of Rhé, offshore from La Rochelle in the Bay of Biscay. A manuscript 'Journall of the voyage of Rease' in the British Library mentions 'John the Dukes Gardiner' as an engineer, describing him as 'best of all this true and most deserving'. It seems hard to imagine that the carnage of La Rochelle could have been turned to any botanical advantage, yet Parkinson and Thomas Johnson agree that the 'greatest Sea Stocke Gilloflower' (probably *Matthiola sinuata*) 'was first sent over from the Isle of

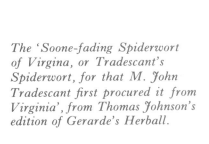

The 'Soone-fading Spiderwort of Virgina, or Tradescant's Spiderwort, for that M. John Tradescant first procured it from Virginia', from Thomas Johnson's edition of Gerarde's Herball.

Rees by Mr. John Tradescant'. Among the curiosities later shown at the Ark were 'A copper Letter-case an inch long, taken in the Isle of Ree with a Letter in it, which was swallowed by a Woman, and found', and a silver medal struck 'Upon the Isle of Ree Voyage', evidently not Tradescant's own since only the French commemorated the occasion with the issue of a medal.

Buckingham's assassination in 1628 robbed Tradescant of his employer but cleared the way for his appointment two years later as 'Keeper of His Majesty's Gardens, Vines and Silkworms' at Oatlands Palace in Surrey, with a handsome salary of £100 a year.

The years that followed must have been particularly full. At this time Tradescant carried out his duties at Oatlands, a rambling edifice built by Henry VIII in 500 acres of parkland and now a favourite resort of Henrietta Maria, while transforming at the same time his own family home at Lambeth (acquired late in 1628 or 1629) into an internationally renowned resort for those interested in all manner of natural and artificial rarities. The garden too benefitted from many gifts of plants sent to Tradescant by friends on the Continent and in North America. Yet in 1637 Tradescant was ready for a new challenge: reaching 'some reasonably good terms of agreement' with the Earl of Danby, he secured the position of first Curator of the Botanic Garden recently founded by Danby at Oxford. The Oxford garden, planted with 'divers simples for the advancement of the faculty of medicine', would have presented somewhat different problems to those which had occupied most of Tradescant's working life in the rose bowers and vegetable gardens of the aristocracy, but his untimely death in 1638 robbed him of the opportunity of crowning his practical gardening career with academic esteem.

Although the name of Tradescant was to be heard again in Oxford, it was in his parish church of St. Mary at Lambeth that John was laid to rest. The churchwardens' accounts for the year 1637-38 record the occasion with the doleful entry: 'Item, John Tradeskin; ye gret bell and black cloth, 5s. 4d.

John Tradescant the Elder by Cornelis de Neve.

The gateway to the Oxford botanic garden

In the place of John Tradescant, his father, deceased

Under the year 1608 the church registers at Meopham bear the record: 'August the iiij daye John the sonne of John Tradescant was baptized eodem die'. No other mention survives from the earliest years of John the younger's life until, at the age of eleven, he was enrolled at the King's School, Canterbury, a stone's throw from Lord Wotton's garden where his father's mandrakes spread their roots. For four years the rudiments of education were instilled in him. An early marriage at the age of nineteen produced a daughter, Frances, and a son, John, who was not himself to survive beyond nineteen years.

There can hardly have been much doubt surrounding the career to be followed by the younger Tradescant and in 1634 he was duly admitted a freeman of the Gardeners Company. The death in that same year of Jane, his first wife, would have cast a cloud over young John's achievement and his father's gratification.

Within three years, further evidence emerges of the son's inclination to emulate his father. The elder Tradescant had been an investor in the Virginia Company, and from a record of 1637 in the State Papers we learn of the first of three visits by the son to Virginia, when 'John Tradescant was in the colony to gather all rarities of flowers, plants, shells, &c'. Parkinson gives further details of some of the botanical trophies carried home from the New World by Tradescant, among them varieties of ferns and reeds, cypress, jasmine and columbine.

On his return from Virginia in 1638, the keepership of the gardens at Oatlands fell to the son 'in the place of

Oatlands Palace from within the main courtyard, by A. van den Wyngaerde, 1559.

John Tradescant, his father, deceased'. Something of the duties he undertook there can be gleaned from a bill preserved in the Ashmolean Library, for expenses relating to 'amending the Walks in the Vineyard Garden, and for Works to be don to the Gardens at Oatlands, and for repaireing the Bowling Greene there'. The security offered by the new appointment may have encouraged

Tradescant's second marriage in October of 1638 to Hester Pookes. Hester was related by marriage to the de Critz family of painters, who were to produce a series of portraits of the Tradescants still preserved at Oxford. John de Critz had been employed contemporaneously with the elder Tradescant at Hatfield and at Oatlands, and their acquaintance may have provided the basis for the young couple's relationship.

John Tradescant the Younger (left) accompanied by Roger Friend, with exotic shells from the Ark.

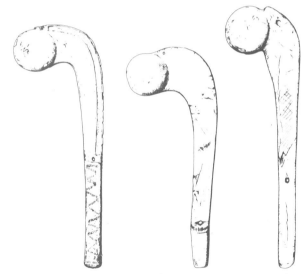

Ball-headed clubs or 'tamahacks' from north-eastern America in the Tradescant Collection.

In June 1650 the Tradescants received the first of many recorded visits from Elias Ashmole and his wife, in the company of Dr Thomas Wharton. Thereafter a friendship developed which led to Ashmole and Wharton collaborating with Tradescant in the preparation of a catalogue of the museum and gardens at Lambeth and ultimately to the inheritance by Ashmole of the rarities from Tradescant's Ark.

9

Rarieties att John Tradescans

Although it is for their botanical prowess that the Tradescants are most widely remembered today, in their own lifetimes it was the museum they developed at Lambeth which brought them particular fame.

The elder Tradescant's all-embracing curiosity has already been mentioned: he was clearly a collector through and through. In his maturing years a fashion had already developed for forming collections or 'cabinets' of curiosities of art and nature, notably among the princes and savants of continental Europe. Normally these constituted adjuncts to the owner's library and admittance was gained only by personal introduction. One of the first such collections Tradescant would have known belonged to Sir Walter Cope, a close friend of the Earl of Salisbury, for whom Tradescant made purchases of plants during his visit to the Low Countries on Salisbury's behalf in 1611. The same journey may also have provided the opportunity for him to see the well-known collections housed in the Physic Garden and in the Anatomy School at Leiden, which were accessible to the public during the summer months. These collections, and others which he may have seen in Paris, could have provided models for Tradescant's own museum —The Ark.

The first we hear of The Ark is in 1634, some six years after the family settled at Lambeth. By that time it was already quite extensive, for when Peter Mundy went 'to view some rarieties att John Tradescans' he spent the whole day 'in peruseing, and that superficially, such as hee had gathered together, as beasts, fowls, fishes, serpents, wormes (reall, although dead and dryed),

pretious stones and other Armes, Coines, shells, fethers, etts. of sundrey Nations ... Curiosities in Carvinge, paintinge ... Medalls of Sondrey sorts, etts'. Many of these items were noted again four years later by a visiting German, Georg Christoph Stirn, whose diary (preserved in the Bodleian Library) also records items of special interest such as 'the Passion of Christ carved very daintily on a plumstone', 'the Pater Noster of Pope Gregory XV', and 'the robe of the King of Virginia'.

Some of the exhibits at Lambeth would certainly have been brought back by the Tradescants from their travels. Some were no doubt acquired from other travellers by way of exchange, much as plant specimens were exchanged between gardeners. Others again were gifts and the

The Tradescants' house at Lambeth (left) in the late 18th century. The frontage dates from the 1620s and the roofline from c.1750.

catalogue of the collections, published in 1656, contains a five-page list of donors ranging from the King and Queen to ships' captains and ordinary citizens. An analysis of this list has suggested that the elder Tradescant had attracted most of the donations, benefitting particularly from his association with the Duke of Buckingham. The son also claimed to have augmented the collection with 'continued diligence': recorded examples of his contributions include an occasion when Henrietta Maria entrusted him with the temporary safekeeping of a fragment of the True Cross (part of this relic, 'which casually had been broken from it', later being 'deteyned' when the Queen reclaimed her loan), and a later purchase of what was believed to be a thigh bone of the Hertfordshire giant, Jack o' Legs, from the church at Weston.

A practical function performed by The Ark was the provision of a remarkable collection of exotic flora and fauna which proved of real value to scholars of the day. Hence John Ray spent some time there studying stuffed birds, notably the dodo, while the illustrations of certain South American fruits in **Thomas Johnson**'s edition of Gerard's *Herball* were made at Lambeth, where the originals were to be seen dried and fashioned into 'morrice bells', as worn by the cannibals.

But the most important feature of the museum was undoubtedly its accessibility, for the Tradescants abandoned the custom of admitting only a privileged few to their cabinet. For a fee, (seemingly 6d. — no small sum in those days), the doors of The Ark were open to anyone and in this the Tradescants heralded a new age for the museum in Britain.

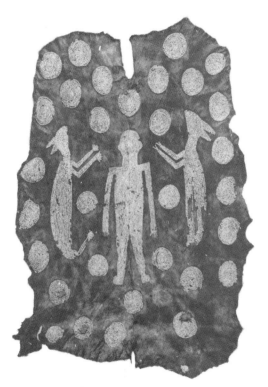

'*Powhatan's Mantle*', *of deer skin and shells, the pride of the Tradescant Collection.*

Virtuoso and curioso

Elias Ashmole, whose name came to be linked with that of the Tradescants both in Lambeth and at Oxford and who came to be described by Anthony Wood as 'the greatest virtuoso and curioso that ever was known or read of in England before his time', began life in modest circumstances in 1617. The son of a Lichfield saddler and of a mother connected with the minor gentry, the young Ashmole showed a combination of talent and assertiveness which were to serve him well throughout his career. By the age of twenty-one, with a legal training and a youthful marriage into the Cheshire squirearchy behind him, he had begun to 'solicit in chancery' in London, being sworn some three years later as an attorney in the Court of Common Pleas. Finding himself out of sympathy with the prevailing political climate, however, the young lawyer soon withdrew again to join his father-in-law in Cheshire. Ashmole's wife Eleanor had in the meantime died in 1641 in her second unsuccessful attempt to bear him an heir.

Three years of contemplative withdrawal were ended when Ashmole received an appointment as a local collector of the newly levied excise duty. When a visit to Oxford arose in this capacity, the seductive appeal of the university and the exigencies of the Civil War conspired to detain him there for a year, combining studies in natural philosophy, mathematics and astronomy with a commission as one of His Majesty's Gentlemen of the Ordnance. The heady mix of scholarship, warfare and high society — for the entire Court was lodged in Oxford at this time — was one which would have been altogether to his liking. In 1646, the year after Ashmole's arrival in Oxford, official duties carried him to Worcester, where he was appointed Receiver of

Elias Ashmole as Windsor Herald, in the funeral procession of the Duke of Albemarle, 1670.

Excise and Controller of Ordnance.

The collapse of the Royalist cause sent him into the wilderness once again. A second marriage in 1649, this time to an aristocratic widow twenty years his senior, relieved Ashmole of the need 'to take paines for a livelyhood in the world' but earned him the enmity of the widow's family, several of whom found themselves the losers in litigation brought by Ashmole in pursuit of various elements of his wife's estate. Under the Restoration, Ashmole finally found himself in a milieu which was entirely to his taste and in which his numerous talents could flourish. Within months of Charles II's return to England, Ashmole was appointed Comptroller of the Excise. Under his authority the revenues doubled over the space of some twenty years.

While Ashmole's administrative flair was successfully exercised in the Excise, his detailed knowledge of genealogy, heraldry and the orders of chivalry brought well-deserved recognition in other quarters. A renewed significance had imbued these matters since the Restoration and Ashmole's exceptional knowledge of them was acknowledged with his appointment in 1660 as Windsor Herald. In 1661, the year in which Ashmole brought out his *Catalogue of the Peers of the Kingdome of England*, the sumptuous coronation of Charles II took place in London. As one of the principal heralds Ashmole would undoubtedly have had a hand in its planning, and the following year he published an account of the 'Solemn Rites and Ceremonies' performed on that occasion. Later, in 1672, the effort of seventeen years of research was crowned with the appearance of his *Institution, Laws & Ceremonies of the most Noble Order of the Garter*. This work of immense scholarship brought Ashmole the unstinted praise of his contemporaries and more tangible tokens of appreciation in the form of gold chains and medals from several of the foreign holders of the Order. Subsequently Ashmole became disillusioned by internal dissension at the College of Arms, resigning the office of Windsor Herald and later declining appointment as Garter King of Arms. Throughout his life, however, he never lost his authority as one of the principal arbiters in heraldic matters.

Elias Ashmole by John Riley. He wears a gold chain and medal presented to him by the Elector of Brandenburg.

Antiquary, astrologer, alchemist

The accomplishment which Ashmole brought to his personal interests was hardly less impressive than that which marked his official roles. A taste for antiquarian studies was perhaps a predictable extension of his enthusiasm for heraldry and genealogy, although the latter were of much more immediate importance to society in Ashmole's day than they are in ours. His particular passions were for books and manuscripts, of which he built up a considerable library, and for numismatics. His expertise with coins and medals had led to invitations to catalogue the Roman collections of the Bodleian Library in 1658 and the royal cabinet in 1660, while his own collections were among the best of their day. Important parts of his collections were lost in a disastrous fire which destroyed his chambers at Middle Temple in 1679: many printed books, gathered together over thirty years and more, were consumed by the flames; a large collection of

Frontispiece to Ashmole's Fasciculus Chemicus with, on the facing page, a horoscope in his hand dated 20 May 1650. This copy was presented by Ashmole to the Bodleian Library.

Flint axe once belonging to Ashmole, from Oldbury, Warwickshire.

wax seals simply melted away and some 9000 coins and medals of copper and silver were reduced to scrap. Other antiquities lost in the fire included a collection of flint implements — perhaps the earliest such collection in

Britain and certainly the first to be appreciated as a potential means for dating early man: one of these had previously been illustrated by Sir William Dugdale, the father of Ashmole's third wife, in his *Antiquities of Warwickshire*.

Less predictable, perhaps, was Ashmole's absorbing interest in alchemy and astrology, pursuits which seem to our eyes quirky and eccentric in a person of Ashmole's standing but which were considered unremarkable in his day. Not a man to trifle with any subject, Ashmole became obsessed with astrological prediction, casting horoscopes before undertaking any action, however minor, reading omens and attempting to establish their outcome, and probing in other ways 'the deepe & hidden courses of Nature'. His reputation for skill in this field may be judged from the fact that Charles II consulted him on more than one occasion.

In alchemy Ashmole and his contemporaries sought a tangible counterpart to the speculative pursuits of astrology, for the aims of this now obscure science were to influence and manipulate the natural forces instead of merely predicting their course. Its aims were not primarily concerned with the material, however, and it was certainly the spiritual, intellectual and historical dimensions of the subject which most attracted Ashmole. Two important alchemical compilations were published under his name: the *Fasciculus Chemicus* of 1650 was a translation of two Latin works by Arthur Dee, while the *Theatrum Chemicum Britannicum* of 1652 formed a compendium of influential but hitherto largely unpublished works by the most authoritative English writers on the subject.

Primary entry in the Ashmolean Museum's Book of Benefactors, with Ashmole's arms.

15

By unhappy law-suits much disturbed

The transfer of the contents of Tradescant's Ark to Elias Ashmole was not to prove a straightforward matter. Before his death in 1662 John Tradescant the younger had sought to supercede the terms of the deed of gift by which Ashmole was to inherit the collection by making a will in which the King was to be offered first refusal of it. In a later will the universities of Oxford or Cambridge were named as the beneficiaries, the choice to be left to Mrs Tradescant who would enjoy the ownership of the collection during her lifetime. No record survives to indicate whether Ashmole became aware of this change of heart before Tradescant's death, but all became clear with the reading of the will in 1662. Faced with the prospect that the extraordinarily important collection might slip through his fingers, a possibility reinforced by claims from Hester that parts of it had already been sold off, Ashmole sought to protect his interest by filing a bill in Chancery against Hester. Two years passed before the case was heard, but in 1664 the court upheld Ashmole's claim on the rarities, the deed of gift by which they had been promised to him being irrevocable without the agreement of both parties. In accordance with the deed, however, the collection was to remain in trust with Hester, a provision which led to further intermittent conflict.

After ten years, during which time the relationship between them was ambivalent enough for Ashmole to store part of his library from Middle Temple with Hester during the Great Fire of 1666 and for Hester to sell off further elements of the collection in 1667, Ashmole took out a lease on the adjacent property at Lambeth. Thereafter relations deteriorated further. Following an attempted robbery at the Tradescant house, the rarities were handed over to Ashmole for safekeeping: Hester contended that Ashmole had harassed her into this action, though she later retracted this claim; according to Ashmole, Hester had been insistent that he should remove the exhibits and he had been persuaded to do so only after she had threatened to throw them into the street. Hester's death finally put an end to all disagreement: she was found drowned in her garden pond on 4 April 1678.

By the time of Hester's demise, the authorities of the University of Oxford had already accepted a proposal that the collection begun by her father-in-law should be given a permanent and indeed honoured resting-place under their

Ashmole's house at Lambeth in the late 18th century. The Tradescant's house adjoins on the left.

Hester Tradescant with her stepchildren, John and Frances.

'It has of a long time been my Desire to give you some testimony of my Duty and filial Respect, to my honoured mother the University of Oxford, and when Mr. Tradescants Collection of Rarities came to my hands, tho I was tempted to part with them for a very considerable Sum of money ... I firmly resolv'd to deposite them no where but with You.'

With the rarities came the Tradescant family portraits, to be hung about the gallery walls. The key role of the Tradescants in amassing the collection was again acknowledged in a Latin poem composed to celebrate the foundation of the Museum, although it was Ashmole's name which the institution adopted.

Today we have many reasons to be grateful for Ashmole's intervention in the history of the Tradescant collection. Without him it seems likely that large parts of the collection would have been dispersed before it ever left Lambeth. But for his academic and social standing it seems improbable that the University would have been persuaded to build a new 'repository' to house the rarities. Without his meticulous attention to detail the comprehensive list of rules by which the museum was to be regulated and its contents protected would have remained unwritten. Most importantly, without Ashmole's conviction that 'the knowledge of Nature is very necessarie to humaine life, health, & conveniences thereof, & because that knowledge cannot be soe well & usefully attain'd, except the history of Nature be knowne & considered', the collection might well have sunk into permanent obscurity. As it was, the rarities were about to be given a whole new lease of life as the focus of scientific effort in Oxford for generations to follow.

care. Although such an idea had been conceived by the younger Tradescant, it was Ashmole who brought it to fruition. His motives were set out in a letter of 1683 addressed to the Vice-Chancellor:

The Ashmolean at Oxford

East front of the original Ashmolean Museum in Broad Street, Oxford, engraved by Michael Burghers c.1685.

In the space of the half century or so which had elapsed since John Tradescant had opened his closet of rarities to the public gaze, a revolution had occurred in scientific thought. This resulted in an entirely new approach to the study of natural phenomena, in which practical experiment and observation replaced the arid theories which had previously formed the basis of the subject. The Royal Society, of which Ashmole was a founder-member, had been to some extent a product of this revolution and the Ashmolean was to be another. The vast body of material which had been gathered by the Tradescants primarily for its rarity value was now prized as a resource for the study of 'several parts of usefull and curious learning', just as Ashmole had anticipated.

One of Ashmole's stipulations in presenting the collection to the University had been that a purpose-built 'repository' should be constructed to house it, preferably with chimnies 'to keep those things aired which stand in need of it'. In the spring of 1679 work began on the new building, a handsome structure designed and built by an Oxford mason, Thomas Wood. The site chosen lay on Broad Street, adjacent to the Sheldonian Theatre (newly built by Sir Christopher Wren). After four years and the expenditure of some £4500 (a vast sum which so depleted the University's coffers that no books could be afforded for the Bodleian Library for some years to come), all the elements of the building were completed. The museum proper was to occupy the first floor, the ground floor being taken up by a lecture hall and the basement by a 'chemical laboratory'.

As first keeper of the Ashmolean Museum (and first

professor of chemistry) the University appointed Dr Robert Plot, whose influential *Natural History of Oxfordshire*, published in 1677, exemplified the integrated approach to the study of nature and antiquity which was to characterise the Ashmolean in its early years. A letter from Plot to Martin Lister, the distinguished naturalist, mentions that on 'Fryday next [16 February 1683] I goe for London to fetch down Mr. Ashmoles Collection towards furnishing this House, when I guess I shall spend about a month in Catalogueing and boxing them up'. Twenty-six large chests were eventually dispatched by barge to Oxford where, on 20 March 1683, Anthony Wood noted in his diary that 'Twelve Cart-loads of Tredeskyns rarities Came from Mr Ashmole' for the new 'Elaboratory'. By the beginning of May, Wood tells us, 'the rarities were all fixed in their distinct cabinets and places, and the roome furnished in every part of it'.

The same author describes the royal opening of the Museum on 21 May 1683, by the Duke of York (soon to be James II), the Duchess Maria Beatrice, and the Princess Anne. Being greeted with a speech from Dr Plot, the royal party was then 'entertained first with rarities in the upper room, and afterwards with a sumptuous banquet there at the charge of ye University. Then they went downe to the Elaboratory, where they saw some experiments to their great satisfaction'. Two days later, 'Yeomen beadles went to several colleges and halls to give notice to all Doctors and Masters that the Musaeum Ashmoleanum would be open the next day'. Some who were greatly taken with the 'new philosophy' delighted in the collections, while others — notably the Christ Church men — saw them as mere

Robert Plot, DCL, FRS, first keeper of the Ashmolean Museum.

baubles and stayed away.

The new school was to win the day, however, and the Ashmolean, with 'the ingenious Dr Plot' at its head, became the principal centre for scientific research within the University.

Britain's oldest public museum

After the excitement of its opening, the Ashmolean settled down to routine life. Plot and his assistant, Edward Lhuyd, set about classifying the exhibits. The Latin catalogues which they compiled between them remain to this day the primary records for many items in the collections.

Lhuyd succeeded Plot as keeper in 1690. Something of the immense range of Lhuyd's scholarship can be gleaned from his principal publications, the *Lithophylacii Britannici Ichnographia* of 1699 and the first volume of *Archaeologia Britannica* of 1707. Lhuyd's *Lithophylacii* is of particular interest, being illustrated with many

Edward Lhuyd, the second keeper, from the Ashmolean Museum's Book of Benefactors.

specimens of fossils from the collections, then one of the principal assets of the Museum.

From 1710 there survives a fascinating account of the Museum, contained in the diary of a travelling German named von Uffenbach. On the whole, von Uffenbach's enthusiasm for the contents of the Museum and for its regulation are somewhat muted. He took particular exception to the way the public conducted themselves: 'even the women are allowed up here for sixpence', he says; 'they run here and there grabbing at everything and taking no rebuff from the *Sub-Custos*'. Only in the matter of Lhuyd's splendid collection of fossils was his praise unstinting, finding them 'faultlessly arranged according to class and species'.

Few of Lhuyd's successors were to match him in stature. The story of the Ashmolean throughout much of the eighteenth century is one of decline, yet the post of keeper was nonetheless hotly contested and accusations of irregular practice surrounded several of the appointments. When Thomas Hearne called at the Museum a month after one of these elections, he found the keeper 'was out of town, and had locked up the door and carried the key with him, being apprehensive his Election would be contested'.

Only occasionally did an exceptional candidate emerge, as when William Huddesford was appointed in 1755 at the age of twenty-three. While Huddesford applied himself with energy to the task of reordering the 'confus'd heap of natural Bodies' he had inherited from his less assiduous predecessors, those who followed him failed to maintain his impetus and the Ashmolean sank into ever greater obscurity.

The ground floor of the Ashmolean Museum c.1836, after the zoological specimens had been redisplayed there.

It took another revolution to break the spell which held the Ashmolean in suspended animation for so long when, in the first half of the nineteenth century, the entire foundations of natural history were shaken by the work of Buckland, Darwin, and others. Under the successive keeperships of the Duncan brothers, the Ashmolean began to reflect something of these events going on in the wider world, with the exhibits being reclassified according to current theories.

Already, however, there had begun a fragmentation of the collections, a process which was to be a major feature of the Ashmolean's nineteenth-century history. First the geological specimens were moved out, to be followed later by the zoological holdings. These were dispatched to the new University Museum, while the coins were sent to the Bodleian Library and the ethnological specimens to the Pitt Rivers Museum. The remaining antiquities were later amalgamated with the paintings and sculpture held in the University Galleries and with them, in 1908, went the institutional title. This is the building known today as the Ashmolean Museum, which contains much of what survives from the Tradescant collection. The original building of 1683 has in the meantime taken on a new lease of life as the Museum of the History of Science, a function which would have found immediate favour with those who contributed to its foundation.

Facade of the University Galleries in Beaumont Street, now the Ashmolean Museum.

Meanwhile at Lambeth...

In the course of the last three centuries far-reaching changes have been wrought on the parish inhabited by Ashmole and the Tradescants. Being overtaken by the expanding boundaries of greater London, the gardens which had nurtured so many rare and exotic species dwindled to a pool of green amongst the encroaching dwellings before finally disappearing under the slate roofs of nineteenth-century housing developments. The nameplate of Tradescant Road stands now in Lambeth on the site of their orchards as a memorial to more auspicious days.

Until recent years congregations at St. Mary's swelled accordingly, with major restoration and remodelling of the medieval structure being undertaken in the mid-eighteenth and mid-nineteenth centuries. In the post-war years, however, St. Mary's had no immunity from the general drift from the Church and finally, in 1972, services were discontinued altogether. Boarding went up over the stained-glass windows, blacking out Ashmole's tomb in the Pelham Chapel. Weeds invaded the churchyard, laying seige to the tomb of the royal gardeners.

It was this vision of dereliction which greeted John and Rosemary Nicholson when their interest in the Tradescants first brought them to St. Mary's in 1974. The feelings of gloom and exasperation they carried away with them on that occasion were crystallized two years later by an announcement that the church was to be demolished. With a number of similarly concerned people drawn about them, the Nicholsons began to formulate plans to rescue St. Mary's from an

Plan of the knot garden opened at St. Mary's on 26 May 1983.

undeservedly undignified fate. An early result was the arrangement of a concert in the church on Twelfth Night, 1977, at which the Friends of the Tradescant Trust were formed, a body which has since grown to a membership of over 2000.

The Silver Jubilee of 1977 provided a preliminary focus for the efforts of the Friends, who resolved that the churchyard at least should be rehabilitated for the royal celebrations. Lorry-loads of rubbish were carted away and swathes of rank grass cut back. Nurserymen responded to the occasion with numerous donations of plants to fill newly-created flower-beds. By the time St. Mary's received a jubilee visit from Her Majesty Queen Elizabeth, the Queen Mother, in July of that year, an instant garden had been created where there had been only desolation. The campaign had been opened with heart-warming success.

By 1983, the year in which the Ashmolean at Oxford celebrated its tercentenary and honoured its founding fathers, the first phase of the battle to save St. Mary's had been won. The initial work in the churchyard had by now been consolidated and, under the direction of the Marchioness of Salisbury (the Trust's first president and a descendant of the elder Tradescant's former patron), a seventeenth-century garden had been recreated around the Tradescants' tomb. On 26 May the garden was formally opened to the public by the Queen Mother, while the Vice-Chancellor of the University of Oxford and the Director of the Ashmolean Museum paid tribute at the tombs of Ashmole and the Tradescants with wreathes of laurel leaves and flowers.

The tomb of the Tradescants in the churchyard at St. Mary's, Lambeth.

A museum of garden history

The salvaging of St. Mary's itself has been a more lengthy operation. A structural survey in 1977 highlighted the most immediate threats to the fabric; approval for the Trust's plans to bring St. Mary's back to life was won from the Church Commissioners and a preliminary appeal for the necessary funds was launched.

Ample evidence of the success of this self-imposed mission is already visible. Once decaying and melancholy, the building now boasts a new roof, secure and weatherproof doors, and reglazed windows. Internally a welcoming ambience has been created: the stonework has been cleaned, a new floor has been laid, and efficient heating and lighting systems have been installed. First steps have been taken towards the establishment of a Museum of Garden History with the installation of a permanent display dedicated to the Tradescants complemented by an increasing number of exhibits relating to the history and practice of gardening. A continuing series of temporary exhibitions and a host of fund-raising events are held throughout the opening season, aiming at a current target of £2,000,000 for the further development of the Museum.

The task facing the Trust remains a daunting one by any standards, but inspired by the example of the 'gardiners to the Rose and Lilly Queen' its members are confident of producing a new 'Ark' in which testimony of the rich inheritance we derive from the Tradescants and from their fellow gardeners is gathered together in a museum where every member of the public will be welcomed. No concept could have been better designed to honour the memory of the family which gave its name to the Tradescant Trust.

St. Mary's Church, Lambeth, with the entrance to Lambeth Palace on the left, by Jane Harding.